CW00480947

FROM THE PEN
OF AN AQUARIAN

Love, hope and darker moments

A R Merrydew

Copyright © 2023 by **A R Merrydew**

All rights reserved. No part of this publication may be reproduced, distributed or transmitted in any form or by any means, without prior written permission.

A R Merrydew
www.armerrydew.com
anthonyrmerrydew@gmail.com

This is a work of fiction. Names, characters, places, and incidents are a product of the author's imagination. Locales and public names are sometimes used for atmospheric purposes. Any resemblance to actual people, living or dead, or to businesses, companies, events, institutions, or locales is completely coincidental.

From the Pen of an Aquarian/A R Merrydew. -- 1st ed.

ISBN 9798387777349

This book is dedicated to those in life whom I have met and by virtue of those encounters, have helped to shape the content herein.

Acknowledgements

My sincere thanks to Matt Maguire at Candescent Press who has supported me continuously during the process of bringing this book to life.

My sincere thanks also to Arran Dutton, Dave Perry and Martin Reeve at Audio Factory. Their support and diligence in preparing the audio version of my book has been magnificent.

'From the Pen of an Aquarian' is a selection of poems that have been written based on personal experiences. As the cover of this book indicates, there in love, hope and darker moments. Should the reader find that association, between the verse and their own journey through life, then I would feel I had accomplished something.

FROM THE PEN
OF AN AQUARIAN

From the Pen of an Aquarian

PART I

'I found love was like an ache inside
So deep you could not sleep'

Strangers

One day she met a stranger
Along life's path he walked her way
She turned to him
These words she spoke
'Will I find love along this way?'
He smiled with eyes as deep as space
He turned and looked behind
'I'm sure if you search hard enough
Then this is what you'll find.
I found love was like a summer's mist
It slipped right through my hand.
I found love life's hardest lesson
I will never understand.
I found love was like a surgeon's knife
It would cut you to the bone.
And when you had been all bled dry
It would leave you all alone.
Then love was like a smiling face
That would lift your soul on high
Then love was like a kiss that made you melt
Just before the words goodbye.
I found love was like an ache inside
So deep you could not sleep
And all your worldly goods you'd trade

But in solitude you'd weep.
I found love was like the strongest drug
It would bring you to the floor
A craving so very deep inside
You would beg for more and more.
I found to late love had three sisters called
Malice, Hate and Spite
They each in turn came visit me
To see me through the night.
'So dear lady,' said the stranger
As he left to pass her by
'Beware these things I've told you
I swear I do not lie'.
She smiled and said 'I know it's true
I know you do not lie
For somewhere on the path I've trod
Love also passed me by.'
'Then we will try,' he said 'To learn from this
And do the best we can
For you are just a woman and I am just a man.'
She took his hand
They turned and left, together now as one
To spend their days in search of love
Beneath the moon and sun.

The Mess Hall

These empty chairs where men would sit
And chatter idly with a smile
No conversations linger here
To war they went
But for a while

So young and keen
To right the wrong
Brave hearts cried out 'We won't be long'
Soon we will be at home again
These empty chairs our long lost friends

Then darkness blessed the battles dawn
No banter now
No time to mourn
Smoke drifts across this stark terrain
Will they see those empty chairs again?

Their time is spent their duty done
They are home at last
But not as one
The mess hall now seems so dimly lit
Those empty chairs where ghosts now sit

Love and Thunder

Time fades the smile it's slipped away
Conversation's short though none today
Two ships are sailing different courses
One cart one track but there are no horses
Let's start again I heard one say
Best intentions true but not today
The mist has cleared a voice is calling
There's more than just the rain that's falling
Embrace the future so take this hand
Together unto the light we'll make our stand
Though empty hearts will never fly
Hunched and broken I watch you cry
The total of my life it seems
Is hidden truths and un-slept dreams
In distant days I will stop and wonder
These day's I've lived of love and thunder

Graylingwell

Beneath these roofs of blue Welsh slate
I walk past walls of brick and lime
Watching as you pass your day
Do you think of me from time to time?
Your days of toil are spent some smiling
Frowns and anger may pass your way
And when your working day is over
I will quietly turn and melt away
There is no warm hearth to beckon
There is no family awaiting my return
Long shadows cast across closed gates
A distant life for which I yearn
To spend just one precious moment
And place my hand upon your arm
To feel life again a human being
My presence would not cause you harm
I will wait for you the same tomorrow
And watch your day and be your host
This window from a world I'm trapped in
Now forever an asylum ghost

Deep Blue

I look out across this empty ocean
Beneath this blue and cloudless sky
The sound of waves call out their chorus
Softly as we pass them by
This timeless place we're moving through
Seems ruled by only moon and sun
When kind your mood you rock my cradle
Then fooled am I to think we're one
When darkened skies abound above me
And fists of surf fly to the air
The spray they leave will sting my face
And remind me I must tread with care
No soothing voice will ever charm you
No sonnet nor a mermaid's smile
When suddenly your angers spent
Then peace is yours but for a while
Sometimes I wish I'd never seen you
Nor smelt your scent upon the wind
This much is true my battles lost
My thoughts of you I cannot rescind
I've sailed across your open spaces
And raced your tides and sometimes won
I've seen your moods your changing faces
But then Deep Blue... I am your son

Ozone

This blue planet that holds us near
To live and die in hope and fear
We rape and plunder for gain and greed
In excess we sow our blighted seed
We rob and steal from defenceless nations
To balance books in corporations
In glass towers so far away
They will have their judgement day
The ground is empty, the spoils are gone
Do you hear the tune? The doomsday song
They've made their profit, and had their fill
This was not the plan, it was not god's will
This blue planet that holds us near
Grows warmer year by year
The sea creeps further up the beach
The lowlands already out of reach
Until that inevitable day
When the human race is washed away
And Mother Nature she will endure
Once our saviour but now our cure

Black Dog

Black dog came again last night
And slept beside my bed
He watched me live the nightmares
That dwell inside my head

He lays beside me through the night
And listens to my tears
In silence he is my company
And shares my darkest fears

Black dog is my only friend
When the night is cold and stark
He never passes judgement
As I blend into the dark

He will come again tomorrow
And stay close by my side
He is my true companion
From him I cannot hide

Lifetimes

She said you will learn new lessons
As each lifetime comes to pass
Some will leave fractured memories
Like shards of broken glass

She taught me the difference
From what is real and what is fake
A string of words like 'I love you'
For hearts they are meant to break

We both made pacts and promises
As in lifetimes lived before
She said we will learn new lessons
But we had both learned nothing more

She said you will learn new lessons
Her words were straight and true
For me, this lifetimes lesson is
Nothing will change for me or you

She taught me to feel exalted
My heart was true and sound
Sentiments fired that turned to ash
Laid down on barren ground

Each life will bring you learning
She said as if she knew
Though on her path it seemed
The learning had failed her too

I learnt of repetition
How love can turn to hate
Misplaced words and statements
Regrets that come to late

She said there are no more lessons
I knew this would be my fate
As in lives I had lived once before
I would no longer see her gate

Albert the Tiger

I once knew a tiger named Albert
And a very fine tiger was he
Albert worked for a Circus in Russia
Then retired to Bexhill on Sea.
Each Monday he would wash all of his laundry
And iron his best tiger skin coat
And when there were general elections
He would dress up and go out to vote.
One day he went up to London
For the Queen he wanted to see
And he fell in love with her corgis
Then ate three of them for his tea.
Now the Queen was less than enamoured
To the Tower she had poor Albert sent
And he languished for years in a miserable cell
Where he had plenty of time to repent.
No one heard again of poor Albert
His fate to this day is unknown
But in pictures of Elizabeth Regina
There's a nice tiger rug in front of her throne.

PART II

'When the reds and golds of autumn left
I barely knew her all'

Jasmine

When Jasmine came
Upon life's breeze
With eyes that smouldered dark
Her voice it carried on the wind
The song of thrush and lark

She smiled for me
A summers smile
That warmed me through the fall
When the reds and golds of autumn left
I barely knew her all

Then winter came
Its icy grip
But the summer smile was mine
I sensed a fear the waters deep
Perhaps now is not our time

You lonely flower
Drifting here
Will you send me on my way?
To think of you when the springtime comes
You perfect summers day

The Promise

I watched the sun this afternoon
It fell and left the sky
I closed my eyes and night time came
The time I live and die
The film inside my head began
Demons walked upon my stage
I awoke in a sea of perspiration
My heart was filled with rage]
I watched the sun this afternoon
It left and said goodbye
I closed my eyes and angel came
I no longer had to hide
I'm coming back from alcohol
These moments I must endure
Better days I believe they lay ahead
Of this I can be sure

Wolf

There were candles on her table
And fire inside her heart
Passion deeper than I was able
She was tearing me apart

She turned to me and smiled
Took my heart and fed it to her pack
She said when you are free and clear
I will give you a new one back

In life somethings are meant to be
I was Icarus falling into the sea
A fiery bird rising from the ashes
She rolled her eyes and flashed her lashes

Wolf had kept her promise to me
Life would never be the same
She took me down from her alter
And I was whole again

Sarah Jane...... Asleep Again

I have a narcoleptic girlfriend
Her name is Sarah Jane
And every time I call her
She falls asleep again

I've tried so hard to keep her awake
Her dog now answers her phone
So I'm learning 'cocker spaniel'
And bribing it with bones

If a bomb went off beside her
She'd sleep through it I am sure
Just turn her head and snuffle
And go back to sleep once more

I even put a firework between
The cheeks of her gorgeous bum
But she blew a little love puff
And sadly spoilt my fun

I have no more ideas left to try
What on earth am I to do
As every time I lay beside her
I become narcoleptic too

So, the moral of this tale of woe
Is cuddle up beneath the duvet so
Hold her tightly in arms and then
Let narcolepsy be my new best friend.

The Carousel

I had an invitation to her carousel
The sky was blue and Monday
Her eyes gave me the message
This was to be a fun day

Around we went a carefree chase
The smile she had upon her face
It filled my heart with loves desire
A sacrifice for her temple pyre

Then the sun began to fade
The carousel now dowsed in shade
Her smile had slipped her eyes were sad
To lose this love that we once had

The carousel it came to rest
In shadows now I do my best
The sun and smile have long since gone
Time to ponder where we went wrong

The carousel will start once more
A new love knocking at her door
The sun and smile will be born again
The pretence of love will remain the same

Lost Causes

Painted bedrooms and hallway walls
Half-finished dreams the curtain falls
Not all is what it seems to be
This empty space that lives in me

The brushes have been put away
To see the light some far off day?
Like me they sit and quietly wait
The future a promise that's all too late

To turn back the clock a dream to be
And complete a task ordained to me
This painter's life will ebb away
Those words that she will never say

Painted bedrooms and hallway walls
Half-finished tears we watched them fall
Some things are not meant to be
The paint has dried for you and me

The Fisherman

Beneath this evening's setting sun
A carpet stretched in shades of blue
I heard the gulls call out your name
They know that I am missing you

Surrounded by ten thousand people
I stand alone this foreign shore
My prayers are for a swifter wind
Then we shall meet again once more

A distant angel waits for me
In patience I must mend my ways
Alone tonight I'll sit and ponder
This emptiness that fills my days

In the morning we'll cast our lines ashore
And point north east across the blue
My heart will soar amongst the clouds
For soon I will be home with you

The Plumber's Ode

If two were four I'd have two more
Oh wouldn't that be great
If I had a five, a one and two
I would have got to number eight.

If I could get to twenty-two
I would be on my way to thirty
Then it wouldn't be to far to go
If my wits do not desert me.

Forty is so round and stout
I would have to pinch myself with doubt
And dare I even mention fifty
Goodness wouldn't that bewitch me.

So why not talk of sixty-two
There's room for growth, a grand or two
And seventy isn't that far away
Now that would really make my day.

There is an art when you negotiate
A place where calculators salivate
So think of a number and times by a few
And I will get that quote to you.

Broken Angels

The fears of every mother
Are held on the wind tonight
The broken wings of angels
Lost in their desperate fight

Look in his eyes with pity
They are lost or so it seems
Echoes haunt this lonely city
Chased by shattered dreams

More harm than good will come
There is thunder in the trees
This mother's world is on her shoulders
And it brings her to her knees

Look in their eyes with pity
And think of them each night
They are stronger than the mountains
Tomorrow hides behind the light

Addiction

My words are gliding over you
They leave my lips in vain
My desperate tears wash over you
They fall like winter rain

There's is nothing left for me to do
I have even asked the moon
So selfish how you squander life
I will mourn your loss too soon

Please release from this anguish
To see a brighter day
Perhaps I can then remember you
When things were not this way

You smile at me with goodbyes
My heart is left to grieve
One day I'm sure we'll meet again
But for now, I must take my leave

The Two of Us

Let me tell you about my pillow
Night times are not a lonely place
My friend never stops his chattering
He is so in my haggard face

I wake up tired and mumble
He's alright he'll sleep all day
I shave my jaw with blood shot eyes
And wonder how we ended up this way

He doesn't pay the rent around here
He never helps to iron our shirts
He drags me into classy restaurants
And eats caviar while I eat dirt

So tonight, I will rest our weary head
As the chatter starts again
One head, two people, no peace for me
This pillow talk is driving me insane

I wish I could leave my friend behind
And elope without him missing me
A moments peace is all I ask
That other voice inside of me

The Bacon Baguette

Dear Hannah I found your text message
From eleven twenty-three
Is it true you have a Bacon Baguette?
In the office there for me

No one ever bought me a breakfast
In all of my life before
So shocked was I by your gesture
I fainted to the floor.

When the manager came and saw my plight
Quick thinking was this fellow
He lifted up my aching head
And used my Baguette as a handy pillow.

But as I turned my head to sleep
My tongue popped out and I began to eat
And when my Baguette it was no more
My head again met with the office floor.

So, the moral of this story
Is plain for all to see
Bacon Baguette's do make useful pillows
But they are better off in me.

Twelve Mile Reach

When I die and my soul is free
Then take me down unto the sea
And on my boat and from this beach
Please sail me out to Twelve Mile Reach

And leave me there for eternity
With the gulls, the wind, the sun and sea
Of all life's lessons it tried to teach
I found contentment there at Twelve Mile Reach

And if by chance you pass this way
Your journey through life's storms and lulls
Take time to stow your lines and leach
And come visit me at Twelve Mile Reach

The Hourglass

These grains of sand have trickled past
Time appears to have stood still
For years I searched to find the strength
The courage and the will
And then at last I heard your voice
My fears drifted far away
We sat and talked We reminisced
It seemed like yesterday
However, did this happen so?
That we should drift apart
To spend these years in solitude
And nurse our broken hearts

Solitary Man

Sometimes I lay awake at night
And dream with eyes wide open
Still familiar faces from my past
My memories cannot be broken

I have missed the chance more than once
To redeem myself before
With an act of self-hatred played out
Life pins me to the floor

This knowing deep inside of me
Born from dreams that linger still
Their dim glow like far off stars
No longer give me the will

For I have seen the future time
I live the past in each and every day
To press on and get there it seems I must
There can be no other way

The horizon will call again at dawn
And I vow to do all I can
Though this lonely battle waits again for me
For I am such a solitary man

PART III

'I'm looking for that eternal peace
That hides behind these clouds'

Journeys End

I'm looking for that eternal peace
That hides behind these clouds
To touch the light and feel the warmth
Beyond these cold black shrouds

This turmoil has all but run its course
A life so lived it died
An unholy sin to bare such a thought
Please forgive me though I've tried

These winter days do beat me down
One more summer shall I see
In God's grace I will place my trust
Where eternity waits for me

Surrounded by familiar faces
Of those who have gone before
I will dwell contented in their embrace
For now and evermore

Long Tomorrows

Another dreary weekend
And I wake up again alone
There's an empty space beside me
Where you had made your home

Well my bird has flown and left me
Her shoes no longer lay upon my floor
My bird has flown and left me
Just like she has before

Grey skies now replace the words
That left my lips in vain
And when the long tomorrows come
All that's left will be the pain

So tonight I dream I will hold you
In my arms again and then
My sanctuary will smile at me
And I will be whole again.

The House of God

The house of God is empty now
He has left and walked away
Tired of watching hopeless men
The ones he cannot save
With the world upon his shoulders
This man he cannot mend
Asking him to answer prayers
Perhaps best I do not send
Lost souls like me are destined
To walk this earth alone
And suffer in our silence
For sins only I must own

That Long Goodbye

She turned and smiled
That long goodbye
Two broken hearts
They wondered why

Such contentment here
So deep this place
No longer holds
That warm embrace

Life's winding path
It led them here
To drown in love
And live in fear

Only shadows now
They stop and stare
That long goodbye
Seems not to care

Those lessons will
In days to come
Live in your heart
And leave you numb

PART IV

'Time now spent to count the cost
Of all this love that I have lost'

The Heart of the Desert

The sand soaks up these desert tears
The arid winds remove my fears
Emotions pass these lonely dunes
No more dancing to another's tune

Dark shadows cast on fallen faces
Broken hearts bleed in distant places
The desert will make them whole again
Not certain how not certain when

The desert smiles at my return
Repeated lessons so hard to learn
Time now spent to count the cost
Of all this love that I have lost

Twin Flames

You smile at me my pulse will race
Our hearts collide this private place
Feelings spill out in random ways
So lonely have I spent my days.

Two flames at last become entwined
Kindled in the halls of time
Forged from lives lived long ago
Emotions only they would know.

Then the flames began to falter
Cancelled out before gods alter?
Destiny now is their time is spent?
Their thoughts reserved in deep repent.

Two embers burn to warm the night
Will they again be bathed in light
Now it's time to wait and see
If these two flames were meant to be.

Closed Heart

I'm leaving you with your nightmares
The ones that lurk inside your head
To hide away in your cosy room
Just pretending to be dead
Those stories that you told me
You have carried them this far
So strong and hard, unyielding
A closed heart is what you are
So full of self-opinion
Of me and all my traits
This love we had
You now allege
Is a love you have come to hate
This man is less than perfect
Though he tried to win your heart
But closed it was by others
Destined to be our failure
Before the very start
My dearest love I will render
Those sweet memories
I hold so dear
Across my heart forever
Of that you have no fear

Mi Hada

I think of you as a butterfly
Though you have a broken wing
You are a songbird nestling in my hand
Scared to take a breath and sing

Perhaps you were a fairy
Who was crushed and died inside
A broken heart bled drop by drop
Until you could not cry

You are bold and yet you are broken
A brave face for all to see
I will never fail to treasure you
You mean all the world to me

My Child

When you came into this world
My heart lifted my lips curled
Just to hold you in my arms
I knew no sorrow

When our fingers they entwined
And your heart it joined with mine
You were my world
There was a bright tomorrow

The seasons they came and went
Too little time with you I spent
Then darkness made its bed
And left me feeling hollow

The child has grown the father too
This enduring love I have for you
Mixed regret, a stream of silver tears
I'm holding hands now with my sorrow

Drowning

I have worn another's head now
For two score year's and ten
The memory of that summer's day
It haunts me now and then

Diamonds stretched across the water
The sounds of eager hearts
To save a friend from drowning
They should have let us part

Across these tears I have wondered
What of the boy I used to be
Memorised in a splash of colour
I am not all I appear to be

Absolution

So here am I
The ghost of a man
His memories doused in tainted tears
Treading water day by day
So bold and yet so full of fear

I have nothing left to give
The will has gone
The futures bleak, no soothing song
It's true I will burn for my past sins
With death, this guilt I can rescind

Then two hearts collided
A chance encounter
They raced in tandem unto the flame
An altered path, the future's brighter?
Life now will never be the same

So here am I
The ghost of a man
Saved by the soothing hand of fate
Love arrived at last on gilded wings
After countless years, but not too late

Dark and Light

For me this road is closed now
In no man's land I dwell
Reflections on a former life
Traded for this perfect hell
Her words they failed to win me
In darkness there is light
The seeds of love have withered now
Tarnished with our perfect blight
A fool I am who wanders on
In no man's land I dwell
In darkness there is comfort
There is loneliness as well

The Price of Love

We played loves game
And it took its toll
Our two broken hearts
They are no longer whole
When the music stopped
The air went still
Such time has past
What lingers still
That distant tower
How memories fade
This empty bed
Where we once laid

Summers Days

I will think of you
From time to time
Those summer days
Our hearts entwined

Your smile its true
Raised up my soul
This love at last
That made me whole

Bitter words blew in
Harsh winters came
Though seasons changed
We remained the same

Lost to treason it seemed
The gallows now await
Mistrust to be my final judge
It clearly sealed my fate

How lost they are
Those summer days
That sunshine now
Seems so far away

In my memory
They will always be
Those halcyon days
You shared with me

Angel

I felt the beat of angel wings
They came to visit me today
The Angel said it's time to go
Now we have to fly away

I turned my head and smiled at you
For the love you had given me
Perhaps we will meet again one day
Our time on earth is done you see

On the wings of an angel
The world faded far away
I would have given anything
To have spent one more precious day

As your arms they released me
One last smile I took with me
Held safely inside my heart
For all of eternity

On the wings of an angel
I soared high into the sky
It left me feeling empty
As we had to say goodbye

With folded wings she turned
And her face I could now see
The angel I had left behind
Had come to join with me

Land of Shadows

They are hiding in the shadows
Her memories of the past
Behind half drawn curtains
And fresh cut kindling wood
The love that failed to last

Bitter tears feed the irony
Thoughts tumble through her brain
She grows emptier
As the nights draw in
He will not return again

The past it was written
In her own carefree hand
Too late the mould was set
In future times quiet moments will
Be laced with deep regret

You

I would talk to you
Until the sun comes up
Across a steel blue bay
I would walk with you
On golden sands
Hand in hand
We would spend our days
In moonlight
I would hold you close
And never let you go
My heart is yours
For evermore
I think you already know
I am drowning in your smile
Once more
Those eyes of crystal glaze
Come swim in me
Your heart is safe
For now
And the rest of your days

Cold Coffees

Trust packed his bag
And closed the door
Snow covered fields
There are no more

Trust is left to ponder
In distant days
What could have been
Had she changed her ways

Rekindled passion maybe
From those days of old
Trust had set the bar
Now their coffees cold

She wastes her words
Like unwanted rain
Trust washed away
It's down the drain

Two minds are set
In different ways
There are no more coffees
Being served today

PART V

'Only memories left to cherish
It's the best of them you take'

Hearts Apart

Cast your shadow in the morning
Leave me sadness in your wake
Only memories left to cherish
It's the best of them you take

Turn and leave your smile behind
Warm and tender hold my hand
Anguish floods my troubled mind
You would never understand

Empty the chair where you once sat
Carried on the wings of doves
Your footsteps they no longer tap
Those wasted words of love

My Lucky Socks

This week I wore my lucky socks
I put them on last Sunday
I had a new job offered me
Only half way through the Monday

On Tuesday I won the lottery
Though it was only two pounds fifty
By Wednesday night an aroma came
And our dog began to sniff me

On Thursday I went to the bank
And I didn't have to queue
Everyone waited outside in the rain
What a strange thing for them to do

This morning I got a fresh pair out
Then stopped to consider and began to doubt
Today is Friday and lottery has to been done
Perhaps I will change them on Saturday
And have one more night of luck and fun

So, the morale of this little story
It would seem plain for all to see
If I'm wearing my lucky socks again next week
Then avoid standing next to me

Hope

I hope the last thing I see in this life
Is my perfect summers day
To guide me through eternity
And see me on my way

I hope when the angels come
They are honest fair and true
I hope that with my final breath
I say that I love you

I hope that you will understand
It was time for us to part
I hope this love that we have shared
Will ease your broken heart

I hope the time we've had together
Means as much to you as me
My princess for eternity
Please wait there just for me

This Night

These stars will be my canopy tonight
My company until the dawn
They will see me through this darkest hour
This absence that I mourn
I cannot see the future now
The deep invites me in
I'm standing on the water's edge
Let my eternity begin
You took my love to quell your sorrow
Your heart you gave to me
And yet here I am alone again
This night spent by the sea

Layer Cake

Another story the tale unfolds
Her airs and graces
The tone so bold
In hindsight soon
She will reflect again
As emptiness arrives
Her only friend

His light has gone
Long steps head away
Beyond the reach
Of her shallow days
Emotions dried upon her shore
This man she loved
Will be no more

Past stories leave a bitter taste
Brief encounters were
In her need for haste
And now there's nothing
The plate is bare
Too late the need
For her to tread with care

Familiar Rooms

The sound of laughter came back today
With eyes shut tight I saw the past
Their faces, names and memories stand
This place of youth will always last
Why do all my roads seem to lead me here?
As if to take account or to see once more
This new future to soon become a past
Some other soul to keep the score
To be this privileged and yet so soon
That I alone would understand
The keeper of this place this womb
To stand once more in these familiar rooms

Crow

Crow looked down upon his world
With eyes as black as night
His heart was strong
His courage bold
To make the future right

He had lived the past before
He knew the coming of the light
Crow pledged to hold those dear
Beneath his wings
And make their lives glow bright

Then from the east the settlers came
Soon the prairie days were gone
Crow watched down from high above
For those who had revered him
He knew it would not be long

Trampled under hoofs and wagon wheels
Soon his followers would disappear
Their way of life had vanished now
The sound of campfire songs
Crow would no longer hear

So Crow sighed and took a breath
And one last look below
Before he spread his wings and flew
Casting shadows down upon
This place he used to know

Silence

Even when we know we're wrong
This mayhem rules our day
Bitter words and careless thoughts
Are brought out again on parade

We make each other suffer
For wrongs too late to right
The bitterness pours out again
Dimming this sacred light

I'm sorry is a vacant phrase
Left empty and without might
Too late to mend a broken heart
In a love that was so right

I will not harbour any grudges
And think of you each day
I will never look behind me
From what I have walked away

I will leave you with a silence
Forever ringing in your ears
Our memories will come to haunt you
Across your fading years

Marks on Paper

I have never used this pen and ink
To win a heart before
These words of verse
When all stood up
Could do that I am sure
These little marks on paper
Are all I have you see
To win the heart of someone who
Means all the world to me.

Hungry Hearts

Their eyes were burning coals
As desire danced deep within
This lifetime spent until now
Just waiting to begin

A union of two lost souls now found
Love clawed at hungry hearts
Those barren years in desperation
Though now they are apart

Fear played that final card
The deck was stacked its true
Those tender moments evaporated
Once shared by me and you

Bared and plain we talked awhile
The future rests and waits
Bless each day, bring me a smile
All maybe not too late

Faith

One small word that comforts me
Through the winter to the spring
It lifts my heart to heaven's door
It makes my spirit sing
Faith will take away the winters snow
Mother nature will rise and then
Faith this word that comforts me
It will save me once again

Memories from a Bed Sit Window

This fragile life I'm walking through
These days spent toiling far away
Their faces now are lost to mist
Will I see them in some distant day?

This fragile life I'm walking through
The road ahead is now unknow
So I turn my collar to the wind
My shoes will find their own way home

This fragile life I'm walking through
Solitude my only friend
Dark and comforting throughout the night
Some bridges you just cannot mend

This fragile life I'm walking through
Where will you take me in the morrow
Another winding path I am sure
I am ready for the sorrow

Mirror Mirror

The mirror greets her face again
The smile has gone
Her eyes are drained
Love has fled to distant places
Regret now fills these empty spaces
Tomorrows promise, the same again
A love now lost that still remains

BLM

Injustice starts with scared black faces
Men with guns compound their plight
Shots ring out a life is taken
Justice served for a broken light
A war is raging under cover
The tabloids play the same old tune
This tune is old please change the record
Just tell the truth and make it soon
The crime of colour an instant verdict
Judge and jury stand behind a gun
A family mourns another sibling
Cut down before his life was run
So proud you are this spangled banner
Flying high upon a lofty pole
Think long and hard and find your conscious
Before you take another soul

Black and White

Everything is black and white
As seen through jaded eyes
The truth that you are seeking
These many years are tissue paper lies

Tears abound remembering days
Of fragile broken hearts
Leave unanswered questions dormant
For fear they tear us both apart

Even when we know we are wrong
This mayhem rules the day
Bitter words and careless thoughts
Are brought out again on parade

We make each other suffer
For wrongs too late to right
The bitterness pours out again
Destroying all that could be right

I'm sorry is a vacant phrase
So empty and without might
Too late to mend these broken hearts
In a love that was so right

The Lady of the Lane

From that very first encounter
The Lady of the Lane
Red wine flowed with summer laughter
Her smile was born again

The promise of brighter days to follow
Rose from those tears and pain
Take each smile and rejoice now
The Lady of the Lane

A shower of a thousand kisses
Summer leaves will fall again
Hearts lifted in a sweet new friendship
The Lady of the Lane

So close and yet so far away
That smile will always remain
Memories cherished in future days
The Lady of Lane

Once upon a Beach

The heavens came alive that night
With a canopy of stars
The weary ocean came home to rest
It had travelled very far

Anticipation touched the air
Two hearts embraced as one
Love was born that perfect night
Before the morning sun

Two souls apart had come to here
So long they had been out of reach
The future lay within their hands
This night once upon a beach

Love Profound

His ring she placed on her finger
She smiled and said at last its home
Her heart beat was in time with mine
Something we have always know
The past left a long time ago
And now we have closed the door
Contentment reined our love profound
In safe hands for evermore

Printed in Great Britain
by Amazon

23463006R00051